When playing for \[...]
against Newcastle in 1986, Alvin Martin scored a hat-trick against three different keepers who played for Newcastle in that match.

The highest score ever recorded in a professional football match was 149-0 when SO l'Emyrne purposely lost the game against AS Adema in 2002 to protest a harsh refereeing decision.

All 149 goals were own goals scored by SO l'Emyrne.

Cristiano Ronaldo has now scored a goal in every minute of a football game throughout his career, scoring most frequently in the 23rd minute of games.

Ryan Giggs holds the record for being the most substituted player in the world, having been substituted 134 times over his career as a player.

Laszlo Kubala is the only player to ever play for three different countries (Argentina, Spain, Columbia) and be recognised by FIFA.

Mark Hughes once played for Bayern Munich and Wales on the same day. After playing for Wales against Czechoslovakia in a Euro 1988 qualifier, he appeared as a Bayern substitute in their second-round cup replay against Borussia Monchengladbach.

At least one Bayern Munich player has played in every World Cup final since 1982.

Each team is allowed to have 11 players on the pitch.

The first live televised match was played between Barnet and Wealdstone on 19 October 1946. The BBC broadcasted this match for twenty minutes of the first half and thirty-five minutes of the second half before it became too dark.

Football was invented in China in 476 BC. Back then, it was known as Cuju.

The English were the first to record a uniform set of rules like forbidding touching the ball with your hands for players.

The last time both European Cup (now Champions League) finalists had no foreign players in their starting XIs was when Celtic (Scottish) played Inter Milan (Italian) in the 1966/67 final.

Brazil have now faced Norway four times but have never won a match against them.

The offside rule in football dates back to the early 19th Century.

The FIFA World Cup, attracting an average of 3.2 billion viewers in 2010, 2014 and 2018, holds the record for being the most-watched overall live event by average on television worldwide in the 21st century.

Created in 1856, Cambridge University A.F.C. has been recognized as the oldest club now playing association football.

Penalties in football were only introduced in 1891.

The Santiago Bernabeu was the first stadium in Europe to host both a UEFA European Championship and FIFA World Cup final.

Hibernian played out a 6-6 draw (normal time) with Motherwell in 2010. Hibernian were leading 6-2 up until the 65th minute.

Before the use of whistles began in 1868, referees used handkerchiefs to the same effect.

The most goals scored by one player in a match is 16, by Stephan Stanis for Racing Club de Lens v Aubry-Asturies in a wartime French Cup game on 13 December 1942.

Martin Palermo missed three penalties for Argentina in their defeat to Colombia at the 1999 Copa America, making him the player to have missed the most penalties in an international football game.

The municipality of Milan purchased the San Siro in 1935.

The fastest goal officially recognised by the FA came during a 2004 amateur match between Cowes Sports Res v Eastleigh Res, and Mark Burrows scored it within just 2.56 seconds of the game.

The average footballer covers an average distance of 9.65 kilometres in every game.

The first-ever basketball game was actually played using a football.

The Merseyside Derby (Everton v Liverpool) has seen more red cards than any other Premier League fixture.

The Merseyside Derby has also been drawn more than any other fixture in the Premier League.

In 2001, football itself was nominated for the Nobel Peace Prize.

In a game between Croatia and Australia at the 2006 World Cup, English referee, Graham Poll, gave three yellow cards to Josep Simunic. Failing to send him off after the first two is widely regarded as one of the most disastrous refereeing performances ever.

Only 8 teams/countries have won the FIFA World Cup after 21 different FIFA World Cup tournaments have been hosted.

The San Siro is shared by both A.C. Milan and Inter Milan.

The Football Club name with the most letters is Nooit Opgeven Altijid Doorsetten Aangenaam Door Vermaak En Nuttig Door Ontspanning Combinatie Breda, or NAC Breda for short.

In 1998, Romanian midfielder Ion Radu was sold from Jiul Petrosani to Valeca for 500kg of pork.

Manchester United are the only team to have won the Premier League three times in a row (as of 2022)

The Allianz Arena used to be home to two Munich clubs: FC Bayern Munich and 1860 Munich. However, Bayern is now the sole tenant.

The first-ever international match recognised by FIFA was played between England and Scotland on the 30th of November, 1872. The match ended 0-0.

European teams have reached the final match in the World Cup every year except for 1930 and 1950.

There is a whole museum to commemorate Cristiano Ronaldo's achievements. Named Museu CR7, it is located at his birthplace in Funchal, Madeira, Portugal.

The largest football stadium in the world is surprisingly located in North Korea, and this is the Rungrado 1st of May Stadium, with a seating capacity of 114,000.

Antoine Griezmann voices Superman in the French version of the LEGO Batman movie.

At around four years old, Angel Di Maria transferred from local side Torito to Rosario Central for the sum of 35 footballs.

In 1985, UEFA placed an indefinite ban on all English clubs from participating in UEFA competitions after some Liverpool fans charged and breached a fence separating them from Juventus fans at the 1985 European Cup final. This resulted in the death of 39 people.

The San Siro was renamed in 1980 after Giuseppe Meazza, a player who played for both Inter and AC Milan. So today, it is officially known as Stadio Giuseppe Meazza.

The youngest ever footballer to feature in a senior international match is Lucas Knecht, who appeared for Nothern Marina Islands at the age of 14 years and 2 days.

He is coached by his older brother, 56-year-old Yasutoshi Miura.

Japanese footballer Kazuyoshi Miura is known to be the oldest footballer to ever play the game professionally (aged 54 in 2021)

In 1996, Eidur Gudjohnsen came on as an Iceland substitute, replacing his father in a friendly against Estonia.

In 2021 as Iceland's assistant manager, he also watched his two sons, Sveinn Aron Gudjohnsen and Andri Lucas Gudjohnsen, combine to score a goal for Iceland.

In 2008, Samuel Keplinger refereed a game between SSV Bobingen and SV Reinhartshuasen in Germany, and he was only 9 years and 303 days old at the time.

Football was first referred to as "the beautiful game" by Stuart Hall, an English football commentator. However, Pele made the phrase popular in 1977.

Substitutions during games were first introduced to the laws of football in 1958.

On the 25th December 1914, soldiers along the Western Front of World War I played football matches with men they were at war with as part of an unofficial Christmas truce to celebrate the festivities.

The longest unbeaten club run was set by Steaua Bucharest. They managed to avoid defeat for 104 consecutive league matches from 1985 to 1989.

The Santiago Bernabeu used to be called Nuevo Estadio Chamartin.

Rogerio Ceni holds the record for being the highest-scoring goalkeeper in football history with 131 career goals.

In 2006, Arsenal fielded a team of 11 players from 11 different nationalities against Hamburger SV. They are the only team to have ever done so in the Champions League.

The San Siro is due to be demolished and replaced by a new stadium ready for 2027

The Santiago Bernabeu was renamed in 1955 to honour the then club president and former player, Santiago Bernabeu.

In 1983, Spain needed 11 goals to qualify for the 1984 UEFA Euros with only one match against Malta left. They went on to beat Malta 12-1.

The number 10 shirt worn by Pele in the 1970 World Cup final was sold for £157,750 in 2002.

At the opening ceremony of San Mames stadium, members of the Athletic Bilbao men's team, women's team and youth academy formed a human chain to each carry a piece of turf and brick from the old stadium to the new.

Only three players have ever scored a hat-trick in the Premier League, FA Cup and Champions League: Yossi Benayoun, Sergio Aguero and Harry Kane.

The most red cards ever in a football game came during a match between Claypole and Victoriano Arenas, where the referee showed 35 red cards to all 22 players and the other 14 to coaching staff and substitutes.

In 1998, all 11 football team members died while playing after being struck by lightning in Kinshasa of the Democratic Republic of Congo. Surprisingly, no member of the opposing team was affected.

Prince William, Duke of Cambridge, is the president of the FA.

The record for longest goal scored from open play in a competitive match is held by goalkeeper, Tom King, who scored from 105 yards (96.01m) for Newport County against Cheltenham Town.

The Igraliste Bajarita football stadium is located between two UNESCO World Heritage Sites, the Kamerlengo castle and the tower of St. Marco.

The longest professional football match in history lasted 3 hours and 23 minutes between Stockport County and Doncaster Rovers on March 30th, 1946.

The 2005 Namibian Cup final between KK Palace and the Civics saw the longest penalty shootout ever recorded in football history with a total of 48 spot kicks.

Norwich City finished the 1992/93 Premier League season in third place but had a goal difference of -4.

Before Sir Alex Ferguson became the Manchester United boss, Aston Villa were a more successful team than United.

Four Hungarian players hold the record for the most appearances in Olympic men's football with all of them appearing 13 times each.

Since Liverpool was founded in 1892, Alisson is the first goalkeeper to ever score a competitive goal for the club.

The largest official attendance ever at a football game came at a match between Uruguay and Brazil at the Maracanā Stadium in 1950 when 199,854 people watched Uruguay lift the World Cup.

Manchester United have won the most matches since the start of the Premier League with over 700 wins.

Liverpool's original kit was blue and white, but that changed in 1896.

As of 2021, Everton have the most losses in Premier League history, with more than 400, but they are closely followed by West Ham.

While Zlatan Ibrahimovic has played for six clubs that have won the Champions League at some point in time, he has never won the Champions League himself.

Camp Nou of FC Barcelona is the biggest stadium in Europe with a capacity of nearly 100,000.

Ronaldo de Lima (Brazilian) also never won the Champions League despite playing for four clubs that did. In 2019, FourFour Two magazine named him the best player to never win the tournament.

Chris Nicholl once scored four goals in a game for Aston Villa against Leicester City - 2 for Villa and 2 own goals for Leicester.

For four different seasons, Thierry Henry was the Premier League's highest goal scorer.

In 2020, Jordan Hadaway was dubbed the world's youngest senior football manager after taking charge of a fifth-tier North West Wales side, Caerwys F.C. in 2019.

A match between Coventry City and Lincoln City was postponed 15 times in 1963 due to bad weather.

Jimmy Rimmer is the only player to have ever won the European Cup with two different English clubs.

Arsenal's match against Sheffield United was the first English League match to be broadcast live on radio.

Dennis Wise won the FA Cup in three different decades: with Wimbledon in 1988 and Chelsea in 1997 and 2000.

Between 3 June 2000 and 5 March 2014, goalkeeper Iker Casillas picked up 112 wins out of a possible 153 while playing international football for Spain.

Footballs are 28 inches in circumference and have stayed at this same size for 120 years.

Celebrity chef, Gordon Ramsay, once trialled for and trained with Rangers but was forced to drop football after an injury that damaged his knee cartilage.

There used to be an old Wembley Stadium which was demolished in 2002 to build the current Wembley Stadium.

In a match between Manchester City Women and Reading Women in 2018, the referee, David McNamara, forgot his coin in the dressing room and then made the captains play a game of rock, paper, scissors to determine who would commence play. The FA later suspended him for 21 days.

Some fans of Diego Maradona started a religion called Iglesia Maradoniana, believing him to be the best player of all time.

Rodrigo Rafael Romero Saldivar has the largest football collection in the world with over 1,230 footballs including balls from the UCL, AFCON, FIFA Men's World Cup and more.

Despite retiring in 2006, Alan Shearer remains the Premier League's highest goal scorer with 260 goals.

The nylon twine that was used to knit the roots of grass together at White Hart Lane is enough to stretch around the world.

Ahn Jung Hwan was kicked out of Perugia FC in Italy after scoring for South Korea against Italy in the 2002 World Cup, eliminating Italy from that tournament.

FC Duruji Kvareli, a Georgian football club team that has ceased to exist, used to have their stadium in an ancient medieval fortress.

In 1949, a Fiat G.212 of the Italian Airlines crashed, and the entire Torino football team on board died.

Gareth Barry holds the record for the most yellow cards ever received by a player in the Premier League with 122.

Bobby Knox became the first-ever substitute to score a goal in the English Football League on the 21st of August 1965 when he scored for Barrow against Wrexham.

Copa PRI Fut7 achieved the largest seven-a-side football tournament in Mexico, with 105,203 participants in 2014.

Bert Trautmann was injured during the 1956 FA Cup final between Manchester City and Birmingham City but played the remainder of the match with a broken neck. At the time, none of the players or officials realised that his neck was broken.

Coventry City have now played in the Premier League, Championship, League 1, League 2, Division 1, Division 2, Division 3, Division 4, Division 3 South and Division 3 North.

The fastest red card in a football match recorded by the FA came on the 8th October 2000 in a match between Cross Farm Park Celtic and Taunton East Reach Rovers when striker, Lee Todd, was shown a red card within two seconds for foul language used when the referee blew his whistle.

Classical composer, Sir Edward Elgar composed one of the first-ever football chants in honour of Wolves' hero, Billy Malpass, back in 1898.

The longest winning streak for a football club belongs to The New Saints Football Club of the Welsh Premier League, with a 27-game winning streak that ended in December 2016.

In women's football, the record holders are Olympique Lyonnais Feminin in France that enjoyed a 41-game winning streak until May 2016.

Peter Cech has kept the most Premier League clean sheets with a record of 202 games without conceding a goal.

Woodford United F.C. holds the longest losing streak after losing 65 consecutive football matches.

In the 1937/38 season of English men's league football, Manchester City became the only team to have ever been relegated from top tier league football while defending the title.

Surprisingly, Manchester City also scored the most goals in that season, but that did not secure their league spot.

Fernando Torres began playing football as a goalkeeper before he tried out as a striker at the age of seven.

Cristiano Ronaldo played for Sporting Lisbon's u16, u18, u19, u21, B team and first-team, all in one season.

Since the Premier League's establishment in 1992, only six teams have never been relegated. These teams are Arsenal, Chelsea, Everton, Liverpool, Manchester United and Tottenham Hotspur.

Robert Lewandowski holds the Bayern Munich record for the most consecutive games scored in.

Fred Everiss holds the record for having the longest managerial reign in charge of a single football club after managing West Bromwich Albion for 45 years and 9 months from 1902 to 1948.

Cristiano Ronaldo holds the record for the most goals scored in international football.

The fastest hat-trick in the Bundesliga was scored by Robert Lewandowski for Bayern Munich against Wolfsburg within 3 minutes and 22 seconds.

He also holds the record for most consecutive games scored in the Bundesliga, with an 11-game goalscoring run between August 16 and November 9, 2019.

Manuel Neuer voiced Frank McCay in the German version of Monsters University.

On January 26, 1967, there was a ceasefire in the Nigerian Civil War after Pele and Santos landed in Nigeria for their game against the Nigerian national team, the Super Eagles.

Having won the Premier League 13 times, Manchester United have now won the Premier League the most. More than 5 times more than any other team in the league.

Gareth Barry has made the most Premier League appearances, with 653.

Derby County finished the 2007/08 Premier League season with 11 points, making them the team with the least points ever at the end of a Premier League season.

On the other hand, Manchester City hold the record for most points at the end of a Premier League season with 100 points at the end of the 2017/18 season.

All winners of the World Cup are only given a cheaper replica of the trophy while FIFA keeps the original.

When Rafael van der Vaart signed for Real Betis in 2015, a clause in his contract prevented him from wearing any sort of red in his boot. Red is the colour of Betis' main rivals, Sevilla.

The oldest coach to coach in a World Cup game was Otto Rehhagel, who was 71 years and 317 days when he managed Greece for their 2010 World Cup match against Argentina.

Alex Song has 27 siblings.

Brian Deane scored the first-ever English Premier League goal for Sheffield United, against Manchester United.

---

7 out of France's top 10 most capped players were on the pitch at the same time for the Euro 2000 final against Italy.

Giuseppe Meazza surprisingly played in four World Cups for Italy without playing in any qualifying match.

As of 2021, James Milner had never lost a Premier League game in which he scored.

Gianfranco Zola got sent of in the 1994 World Cup Round of 16 match for Italy against Nigeria on his birthday. This was his first and last World Cup appearance.

Pele has won more World Cups than any other player, winning three with the Brazil national team over his playing career.

Over the course of 70 Premier League appearances, Mario Balotelli managed to make just one assist. It set up Aguero to score the title-winning goal in 2012.

The most remarkable comeback in history is arguably believed to have happened in a match between Charlton and Huddersfield. Charlton, playing with only ten men for most of the match, were 5 down in the 63rd minute but came back to lead 6-5 at the 81st minute. Huddersfield drew level with 5 minutes to play, but Charlton then won it 7-6 with a last-second header.

For eight seasons, Wolfsburg's coach was a man named Wolfgang Wolf.

On the 23rd of September, 2000, Wycombe Wanderers scored two goals in nine seconds against Peterborough United.

During World War II, Old Trafford was claimed by the army and was turned into a depot. As a result, it was bombed heavily during that period.

Cristiano Ronaldo has now scored against more than 120 different clubs over the course of his career.

Americans and Canadians actually refer to football as Soccer.

Italy set the world record for the longest international unbeaten run after staying unbeaten in 37 consecutive international games.

On January 8th 1994, Michael Laudrup helped Barcelona to a 5-0 win over Real Madrid, and 364 days later he helped Real Madrid to a 5-0 win over Barcelona.

In 1994, Andres Escobar, a Colombian football player, was shot and killed in his hometown after scoring an own goal in the World Cup that contributed to Colombia's elimination from the tournament.

A war between El Salvador and Honduras began from tensions and riots that resulted from a qualifier game for the 1970 World Cup. The "war" lasted only 5 days.

Wayne Rooney, Gareth Bale and Kevin Davies are the only players ever to score, assist and score an own goal in a Premier League game.

Andrew Watson is considered the first black player to play football at an international level. He played three matches for Scotland between 1881 and 1882.

Alan Shearer has scored the most Premier League penalties (56) but has also missed the most (11).

The English Football Association has its headquarters based in Wembley Stadium, London.

From 23rd July to 20th November 2011, FC Tom Tomsk, a Russian team, played 1115 minutes of football without scoring a single goal – the longest goalless streak ever.

Liverpool fans can be heard singing "You'll Never Walk Alone" on Pink Floyd's Fearless song.

The original name for Liverpool was to be Everton Athletic, but the FA refused to acknowledge the club as Everton.

The most capped international player remains Soh Chin Ann of Malaysia who captained the international team 195 times.

The Allianz Arena is the first stadium in the world with a full colour-changing exterior.

The most common scoreline in football is 1-1, with 11% of all games ending with that result.

Emmanuel Adebayor has recorded the most offsides in Premier League history. He was caught offside 328 times.

Arthur Conan Doyle, a British writer and physician best known for his very famous Sherlock Holmes series, once played as a goalkeeper for Portsmouth under the pseudonym A.C. Smith.

Peter Crouch has scored more headed goals (53), than 16 of the teams who have played in the Premier League.

The youngest player to ever have 100 international caps is Cha Bum-Kun, who achieved this milestone with South Korea aged 24 years and 139 days.

A 19-year-old, Aldyr Schlee, won a newspaper contest to design the iconic yellow Brazil kit we all know today.

This happened after the previous kit became unlucky following a 2-1 defeat in the 1950 World Cup final.

The World Cup's highest goal scorer remains Miroslav Klose with 16 goals after 24 matches.

The highest ever attendance at Old Trafford, came during a game between Wolves and Grimsby Town in 1939. The match had 76,962 spectators in attendance.

Salzburg player Jonathan Soriano missed the first half of a match against Wolfsberger AC to attend the birth of his daughter in 2013. He arrived in time for the second half, then scored a hat-trick.

Goal nets were introduced to the FA's rules of the game in 1891.

Arsenal tried to sign Lionel Messi alongside Cesc Fabregas from Barcelona's academy.

Arsenal also almost signed Ronaldinho in 2001, but the player could not get a work permit.

The first female football referee, was a Turkish woman named Drahsan Arda, who officiated her first game in 1968.

Richard Wright won a title medal with Manchester City in 2014 despite never appearing for them once.

It's believed that the loudest football ground in the world is the Turk Telecom Arena of Galatasaray in Turkey.

The fans once hit 131 decibels, which is acknowledged as the loudest in Guinness Book of World Records.

Italian clubs have produced 14 different Ballon d'Or winners, which is more than any other league has managed.

FIFA has more member countries than even the United Nations.

The North Korean government handpicked Chinese volunteers to act as fans when the national team played in the World Cup.

The most expensive women's footballer is Pernille Mosegaard Harder who moved to Chelsea from Wolfsburg in 2020.

The Signal Iduna Park holds the European record for average fan attendance.

The South Bank of the Signal Iduna Park is also the largest terrace for standing spectators in European football.

Manchester United retain the record for most successive Champions League games without defeat which is a 25-game unbeaten streak that ended in 2009.

Over 300 people died in a riot after the referee nullified a goal during a match between Peru and Argentina at the Tokyo 1964 Olympics.

Tim Howard has made the most saves in a FIFA World Cup match with 16 against Belgium in the Round of 16 stage at the 2014 tournament.

Manchester United have not always had that name. They started as Newton Heath LYR Football Club. The LYR stood for Lancashire and Yorkshire Railway, one of the major British railway companies of the time.

To clear some debt, the club captain, Harry Stafford, encouraged four local businessmen to invest in the club in return for a direct interest in running it. That led to the renaming of the club.

Terry Connor is the only manager to ever oversee more than 10 Premier League games without winning a single one.

The Isles of Scilly Football League is the smallest league in the world, with just two teams that play 17 times in a season to determine the league winners.

Hulk's total combined transfer fees have now surpassed €100 million, despite not playing in any of Europe's top 5 leagues.

A player cannot be offside from a goal kick in football.

Sadio Mane scored the fastest Premier League hat-trick, netting all three goals within 176 seconds.

The youngest player to ever score a goal and assist one in the same La Liga match is Ansu Fati in 2019 for Barcelona aged 16 years and 318 days.

In 1994, Paul Peschisolido was sold to Stoke by the then-managing director of Birmingham, Karren Brady, for £400,000. He then married Karren Brady the following year.

Jose Luis Chilavert is the only goalkeeper to ever score a hat-trick in professional football, after scoring 3 penalties in a 6-1 thrashing in 1999.

Arsenal are still the only team to go an entire Premier League season (2003/04) without suffering a defeat.

Gary Lineker pooed himself at the 1990 World Cup in a match for England against Ireland.

The all-time leading goalscorer in La Liga is Lionel Messi, with 474 goals.

After decades of bringing celery to Stamford Bridge - most likely to pay homage to their chant "Celery"- Chelsea fans were prohibited from continuing to do so by the club in 2007.

In 1999, Sunderland included a clause in Stefan Schwarz's contract to prevent him from being a passenger on one of the first commercial flights to space

---

Inter Milan player, Javier Zanetti, did not miss a single league game for the club between October 28, 2006, and December 13, 2009.

As of 2018, of the 89 possible trophies that could have been won in Spanish club football since 1929, Real Madrid and Barcelona have won 60.

The oldest football ground in the world is Sandygate (belonging to Hallam F.C.). It was first opened in 1804, and the first competitive game played there was against Sheffield F.C. in 1860.

Only three teams, Athletic Bilbao, FC Barcelona and Real Madrid, have never been relegated from La Liga.

The Norway Cup, a tournament for boys and girls aged 10-19, is technically the world's largest football tournament, with an average of 1450 teams from 50 nations participating each year.

The first-ever World Cup goal was scored by Lucien Laurent at the 1930 World Cup.

Alex Ferguson holds the British record for most games as a manager, having managed 2155 competitive games.

The oldest ongoing football competition in the world is the FA Cup, established in 1871.

In 2006, Juventus were stripped of the Serie A title and relegated to Serie B after they were found guilty - along with some other clubs - of bribing referees and referee associations.

Zlatan Ibrahimovic stole bicycles when he was much younger after a bicycle that meant a lot to him was also stolen.

Lionel Messi has scored the most goals by a single player in a calendar year after netting 91 goals in 2012.

Diego Maradona once used his hand to score a goal to help Argentina beat England in the 1986 World Cup. The referee failed to notice and allowed the goal. This goal has been dubbed the "Hand of God".

The oldest player to captain a Champions League match is Paolo Maldini, who captained in a 2008 CL match for AC Milan against Arsenal aged 39 years and 239 days.

As of 2018, Manchester United were the most valuable football club in the world.

The city of Lusail, which is supposed to host most of the Qatar 2022 World Cup matches, did not initially exist. It was built from scratch, mainly to host the World Cup.

Former Colombian defender, Gerardo Bedoya, was shown the most red cards in football history, with 46.

Ronaldinho lost a $750,000 Coca-Cola sponsorship in 2012 after drinking from a can of Pepsi at a press conference.

Real Madrid is the most successful club in Europe

In 1937, a match between Chelsea and Charlton was stopped after an hour because of fog, but the Charlton goalkeeper stayed on an extra 20 mins because he didn't know the game had been stopped.

Chelsea hijacked Willian's transfer to Tottenham and signed him themselves in the last minute while the Tottenham chairman was trying to get a cheaper deal.

Brazil is still the only country to have won the World Cup five times.

Manchester United lost their opening game at Old Trafford to Liverpool 4-3.

While celebrating a 77th-minute goal for Ipswich against Arsenal in a 1978 FA Cup tie, Roger Osborne was so overcome with emotion that he fainted and had to be substituted.

Former Manchester United coach, Tommy Docherty, was sacked for having an affair with the United physiotherapist's wife. After the affair became public knowledge and his wife left him, he then married her.

In a bid to sign him, Tottenham paid Emmanuel Petit's fare for the taxi that he took to meet Arsene Wenger. After the meeting with Wenger, he then signed with Arsenal.

No English manager has ever won the Premier League.

Miguel Angel Nadal, the uncle of the world-famous tennis player Rafael Nadal, once played for Barcelona.

Crossbars only became a mandatory addition to goals in 1882.

Only 6 teams wear a UEFA badge of honour for winning the European Cup/Champions League five times, or three times in a row: Real Madrid, Barcelona, AC Milan, Bayern, Liverpool and Ajax.

Guillermo Stabile was the highest goalscorer at the 1930 World Cup, even though he wasn't initially on the Argentinian first team. He was also never again called up to play for Argentina.

The Brazil national team's first official match was against the English club, Exeter City.

Ken Aston, a referee, was the first to use red and yellow cards in football to help players see what he was doing through fogs.

In 2006, the Saudi Telecom Company sponsored all twelve teams of the first division in Saudi Arabia.

The longest ever football match lasted 169 hours in a bid to raise funds for a charity, Kicking Off Against Cancer.

In 2016, Manoj Mishra travelled 49.17 km with a football balanced on his head.

Despite making only 9 appearances and scoring no goals for Juventus, Nicklas Bendtner surprisingly has the same number of Serie A titles as Francesco Totti (1 title).

Juventus also failed to sell a single Bendtner shirt during his season there, and when former England cricketer Darren Gough tried to buy one, the shop staff actively tried to talk him out of it.

Arsenal hold the record for the longest unbeaten streak in the English top flight.

The youngest goalscorer in the Premier League is James Vaughan, who scored for Everton against Crystal Palace aged 16 years and 270 days.

Zlatan Ibrahimovic refused to trial with Arsenal at age 16, claiming "Zlatan does not do auditions".

The fastest World Cup goal came at the 2002 World Cup when Turkey international, Hakan Sukur, scored against South Korea after 11 seconds in the third place play-off.

In a 1945 Arsenal friendly against Dynamo Moscow, there was fog so heavy that spectators claim that, at one point, both teams were playing with more than 11 players.

In 1975, Brian Clough lasted only 44 days as a manager in charge of Leeds United.

Romanian international, Adrian Mutu, once posted a picture on Facebook comparing his national team coach, Victor Piturca, to Mr Bean. This led to him being banned from playing for Romania.

Lionel Messi used to play keepy-uppies for ice cream. For every 100 he did, his coach rewarded him with a cone of ice cream.

Lionel Messi has also scored the most goals for a single club, with 672 goals in 778 games for Barcelona.

Sheffield United could have signed a 17-year-old Diego Maradona but did not want to pay over £200,000 for him.

Three women were nominated for the Puskas award in 2019, but no woman has won it yet.

In the very first FA Cup competition, Queen's Park (a Scottish team) reached the semi-finals without playing any matches after their opponents either withdrew from the competition or could not get a venue to play.

Queen's Park then also had to withdraw from the semi-final after they could not afford train tickets back to London for a Wanderers replay.

Surprisingly, over 2% of all the goals scored at the World Cup are own goals.

In 2017, a Woman's Football match was played on the volcanic crater of Mount Kilimanjaro in Tanzania. This remains the football game to have been played at the highest altitude ever of 5,714 metres.

Didier Drogba helped bring peace to his country and stop a 5-year civil war when the Ivory Coast qualified for the World Cup for the first time in 2005.

Dele Alli holds the world record for the most nutmegs in 30 seconds, after completing 8 within that timeframe.

Ajax is named after the Greek mythological hero, Ajax the Great, who died unconquered.

Although they have football as their national sport, Greenland cannot join FIFA or UEFA because they do not have enough grass to play on.

In 2009, AFC GOP player, Levi Foster, got a yellow card before kick-off for farting in the referee's face while having his boots checked. AFC GOP won that match 5-0, and Levi was named Man of the Match.

On his Premier League debut, Ledley King scored a goal within just 9 seconds for Tottenham against Bradford City in 2000.

As of 2021, Manchester United are still the most successful club in England with 66 trophies. Liverpool are a close second with 65.

In the 1980 Copa Del Rey final, Real Madrid faced their reserve team, Real Madrid Castilla. The senior team won the match 6-1.

Jurgen Klopp is, surprisingly, 6ft 4in tall.

The Russian Premier League takes a three-month winter break from mid-December to mid-March because it is always almost impossible to play in the freezing temperatures.

Kylian Mbappe is the youngest player in Champions League history to score 30 goals.

Simon Mignolet, the former Liverpool goalkeeper, actually has a degree in political science and can speak four languages.

Romelu Lukaku also speaks 9 languages: French, German, English, Spanish, Portuguese, Dutch, Flemish, Italian and the Bantu language of Lingala in Congo.

Dundee United (a Scottish Premiership club) has a 100% win record against FC Barcelona after facing and beating Barcelona on four different occasions.

In 1993, Ronaldinho's youth team, Gremio, beat another team 23-0 and Ronaldinho scored every goal.

Gary Lineker was famously substituted off in his last ever match for England when he needed just one more goal to match Bobby Charlton's record as the highest goalscorer for England at the time.

Chilean side, Deportes Arica, commissioned a witch in 2001 to cast out evil spirits and prevent their side from being relegated.

The most viewed domestic football league globally is the Premier League.

While playing for Tottenham Hotspur, Danish international, Allan Nielsen, suffered an injury after his daughter poked him in the eye.

Robert Lewandowski almost signed for Blackburn Rovers in 2010, but a cloud of volcanic ash prevented his plane from taking off.

The youngest coach to ever coach a World Cup game is Juan Jose Tramutola who co-managed Argentina at the 1930 World Cup at just 27 years old.

In a bid to get stripes that wouldn't fade quickly, Juventus wore Notts County (an English side) stripes back in 1903. Since then, they have continued to play in the black and white colours that they are now famous for.

The youngest player to ever captain in the Champions League is Ruben Neves, who captained Porto in a 2-0 Champions League win over Maccabi Tel Aviv at the age of 18 years and 221 days in 2015.

Cristiano Ronaldo scored the 4000th La Liga goal in official competition at the Santigo Bernabeu in a match that Real Madrid won against Levante UD 4-2.

Anfield stadium used to belong to Everton FC until a rent dispute.

Wembley Stadium holds the record for the most toilets in any venue, with 2,618 toilets in the building.

Cristiano Ronaldo is now the highest goalscorer of all time.

Blackburn Rovers turned down the opportunity to sign Zinedine Zidane because they had Tim Sherwood.

Newcastle also turned him down because the club authorities believed he was not good enough for the Premier League.

FC Barcelona was formed after a Swiss football enthusiast, Joan Gamper, placed an ad in the Spanish newspaper "Los Deportes" with his idea of forming a new football club.

Old Trafford is referred to as the Theatre of Dreams because, despite being a football club started by railway workers who were relegated over and over for decades, they never lost the dream to be the best.

The lowest attendance ever in an English league football game was when Thames AFC played a Division Three South game with Luton, and only 469 people showed up to watch.

In 1993, Congleton was holding a minute's silence before the match to mourn the club's oldest fan, who had reportedly passed away during the week when the fan walked into the ground. Apparently, he was not dead yet.

Harry Wilson's grandfather once bet £50 that Harry would play international football for Wales. Once he was called up, his grandfather won £125,000 and retired the next day.

Oliver Kahn, former Bayern Munich and Germany goalkeeper, once played in a penalty shootout against 9-year-olds, and for every penalty scored by the children, money was to be donated to charity. Kahn ended up saving every penalty.

In 1998, English referee Martin Sylvester showed a red card to himself after punching a player.

Lionel Messi is the highest goal scorer in El Classico, with 26 goals from El Classico meetings.

The oldest known football in the world was created between 1540 and 1570, and it was found during a mid-1970s excavation project at Stirling Castle in Scotland.

Giroud's famous scorpion kick for Arsenal won the Puskas award but did not win the Premier League Goal of the Month award for the month he scored it.

The full name of Serie A is Lega Nazionale Professionisti Serie A.

Dusan Tadic now holds the world record for most assists in a calendar year with 37 assists in 2021.

Thomas Langu Sweswe, while playing for Kaizer Chiefs F.C., once played for 90 minutes without touching the ball once.

Spain won the 2010 World Cup but scored only 8 goals throughout the whole tournament.

Philipp Lahm played a total of 765 career games and never got a red card.

The Albanian national team was once detained at London's Heathrow airport after taking £2,500 worth of merchandise from a duty-free shop, misunderstanding the term "duty-free".

Ciro Immobile once refereed a charity match between Lazio's employees and a team from the Vatican at the request of Pope Francis.

The Maracanã stadium's official name is Estadio Journalista Mario Filho after a journalist who pushed for its construction. But it gets its popular name from the Maracanã neighbourhood where it is located.

Bolton Wanderers forward Wilberforce Montgomery once suffered a concussion after a pie was thrown at him during a friendly at Wigan.

Printed in Great Britain
by Amazon

81506832R00059